WORLD'S LONGEST-LIVING ANIMALS

400-YEAR-OLD
SHARKS!

By Joni Kelly

Gareth Stevens
PUBLISHING

Please visit our website, www.garethstevens.com. For a free color catalog of all our high-quality books, call toll free 1-800-542-2595 or fax 1-877-542-2596.

Cataloging-in-Publication Data

Names: Kelly, Joni.
Title: 400-year-old sharks! / Joni Kelly.
Description: New York : Gareth Stevens Publishing, 2019. | Series: World's longest-living animals | Includes index.
Identifiers: LCCN ISBN 9781538217207 (pbk.) | ISBN 9781538216866 (library bound) | ISBN 9781538216873 (6 pack)
Subjects: LCSH: Sharks–Juvenile literature.
Classification: LCC QL638.9 K45 2019 | DDC 597.3–dc23

Published in 2019 by
Gareth Stevens Publishing
111 East 14th Street, Suite 349
New York, NY 10003

Copyright © 2019 Gareth Stevens Publishing

Designer: Andrea Davison-Bartolotta and Laura Bowen
Editor: Joan Stoltman

Photo credits: Cover, pp. 1, 7 Paul Nicklen/National Geographic/Getty Images; pp. 2–24 (background) Dmitrieva Olga/Shutterstock.com; p. 5 (shark) Dorling Kindersley/Getty Images; p. 5 (car) Rawpixel.com/Shutterstock.com; p. 5 (horse) Abramova Kseniya/Shutterstock.com; pp. 9, 19 Franco Banfi/WaterFrame/ Getty Images; p. 13 Richard Ellis/Science Source/Getty Images; p. 15 Incredible Arctic/ Shutterstock.com; p. 17 (kelp) divedog/Shutterstock.com; p. 17 (jellyfish) Norman Chan/ Shutterstock.com; p. 17 (dolphin) Tory Kallman/Shutterstock.com; p. 17 (seal) Dmytro Pylypenko/Shutterstock.com; p. 21 Flickr upload bot/Wikimedia Commons.

Printed in the United States of America

CPSIA compliance information: Batch #CS18GS: For further information contact Gareth Stevens, New York, New York at 1-800-542-2595.

CONTENTS

Boldface words appear in the glossary.

Large and in Charge

It's the largest fish in the **Arctic** and the second-largest shark in the world. It can live longer than any other **vertebrate**. It's the Greenland shark! These mud-colored sharks can grow 24 feet (7 m) long and weigh 2,645 pounds (1,200 kg)!

HOW BIG IS A GREENLAND SHARK?

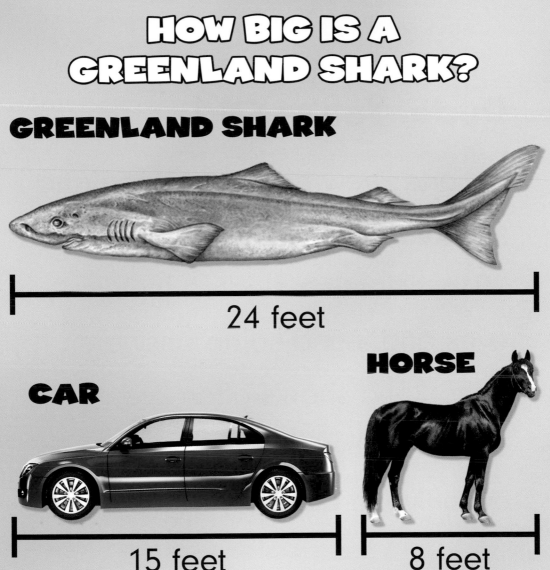

GREENLAND SHARK

24 feet

CAR

15 feet

HORSE

8 feet

Dude, You're Old

No one knew how old Greenland sharks were for years. Then, in 2016, **scientists** studied their eyes and found some answers. Greenland sharks often live almost 300 years! Some may even live to be 500 years old!

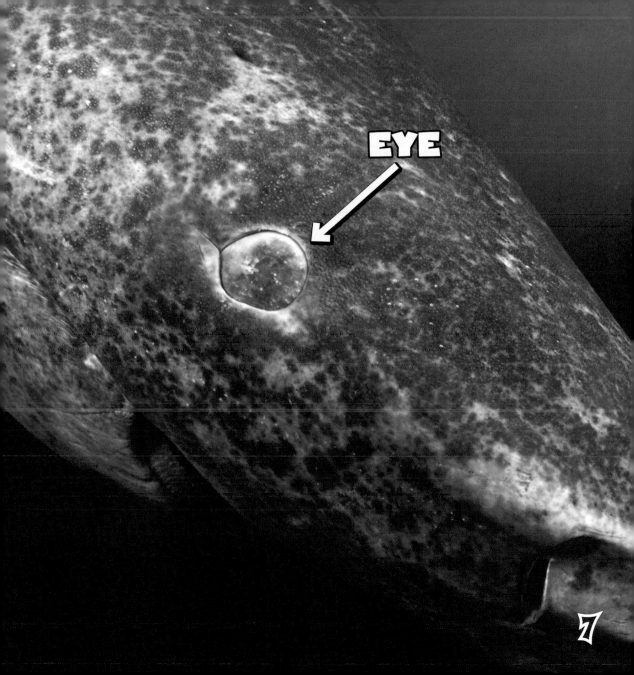

It's hard to get an exact age using today's science tools. One day, we'll hopefully know more, including how Greenland sharks live so long! Part of how they live long is that they have toxic **flesh**, so they can't be eaten. Their size helps, too—they're too big to eat!

Home, Sweet Home

Greenland sharks live farther north than any other shark. In fact, they're the only shark that can live in the cold waters of the Arctic all year round. Their home is so cold that it makes these sharks hard to study—or even see!

GREENLAND SHARK RANGE MAP

Arctic
Ocean

Greenland

North
America

Atlantic
Ocean

Europe

Asia

Africa

South
America

Indian
Ocean

Australia

Pacific
Ocean

Greenland sharks like water that's only 30°F to 50°F (-1°C to 10°C). To find cold throughout the year, they live deeper during summer—sometimes over a mile (1.6 km) deep! In winter, Greenland sharks move up—sometimes even coming to the **surface**!

Most sharks stay away from cold. Greenland sharks may actually live longer because of how cold their home is. Many creatures that live in the deep, cold sea live for a long time! Cold slows down life **processes**, saving **energy** and allowing cells to live longer.

ARCTIC OCEAN

Chow Time!

Another way Greenland sharks can live so long is that they eat anything—dead or alive! They've even eaten reindeer, horses, and polar bears. Scientists think these large animals probably fell into the water and died, but can't rule out that Greenland sharks may be hunters!

A GREENLAND SHARK'S FAVORITE FOODS

KELP

JELLYFISH

DOLPHIN

SEAL

The Arctic Food Web

Greenland sharks are at the top of the Arctic food web. This means they're a very important part of that **ecosystem**. So scientists need to find answers. How many are there? Do they live wherever there's cold water? How many young do they have?

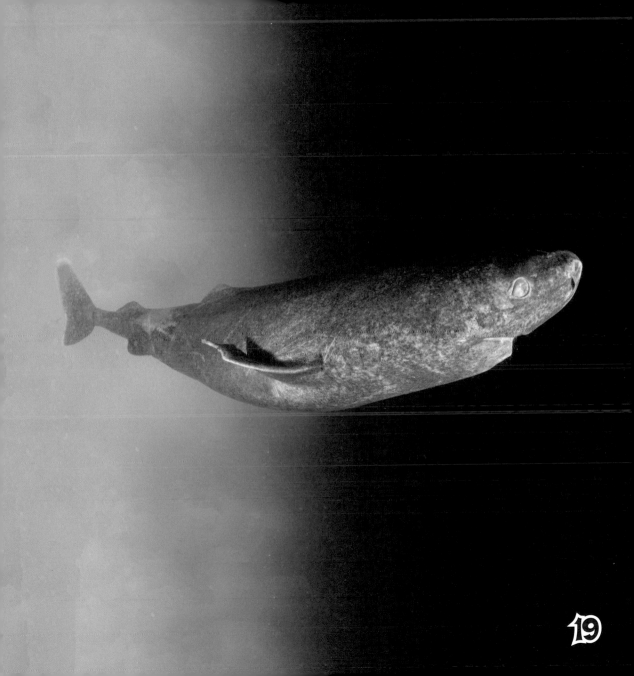

19

Save the Greenland Sharks!

From around 1850 to 1960, 50,000 Greenland sharks were caught every year to make oil. Because they grow so slowly, their **population** still hasn't come back. Greenland sharks may die out before scientists discover how they live so long!

GLOSSARY

Arctic: the North Pole and the area around it

ecosystem: all the living things in an area

energy: power used to do work

flesh: the soft parts of the body of an animal

population: the number of animals of the same kind that live in a place

process: to move something forward in a set of steps

scientist: someone who studies the way things work and the way things are

surface: the top amount of something

vertebrate: an animal that has a backbone

FOR MORE INFORMATION

BOOKS

Antill, Sara. *A Shark's Life.* New York, NY: PowerKids Press, 2012.

Brown, Laaren. *Super Sharks.* New York, NY: Scholastic Inc., 2016.

Discovery Communications. *Sharkopedia: The Complete Guide to Everything Shark.* Des Moines, IA: Time Home Entertainment, 2013.

WEBSITES

The Greenland Shark
sharksider.com/greenland-shark/
Read about the Greenland shark's fins, teeth, eyes, and more.

The Greenland Shark: An Icy Mystery
sharkopedia.discovery.com/types-of-sharks/greenland-shark/
Check out this site filled with pictures and cool facts about the Greenland shark.

INDEX